Dear Teacher... I may forget what you said, but I'll never forget how you made me FEEL

A JOURNAL

It takes a big heart to help shape little minds.

The influence of a good teacher can never be erased.

An Awesome teacher is hard to find, difficult to part with and
impossible to forget.

A teacher takes a hand, opens a mind and touches a heart.

I'm a teacher. What's your Superpower?

Thank you for helping me grow.

The thankful receiver bears a plentiful harvest.

— *William Blake*

No act of kindness, no matter how small, is ever wasted.

— Aesop

Happiness is not an ideal of reason, but of imagination.

— *Immanuel Kant*

Never give up, for that is just the place and time that the tide will turn.

— *Harriet Beecher Stowe*

Happiness depends upon ourselves.

— *Aristotle*

Nobody can bring you peace but yourself.

— *Ralph Waldo Emerson*

Adventure is worthwhile.

— Aesop

The way to know life is to love many things.

— *Vincent Van Gogh*

Wisdom begins in wonder.

— *Socrates*

Quality is never an accident. It is always the result of intelligent effort.

— John Ruskin

The journey of a thousand miles begins with one step.

— *Lao Tzu*

There is only one way to happiness and that is to cease worrying about things which are beyond the power of our will.

— *Epictetus*

This world is but a canvas to our imagination.

— *Henry David Thoreau*

When it is obvious that the goals cannot be reached, don't adjust the goals,
adjust the action steps.

— *Confucius*

Our best successes often come after our greatest disappointments.

— Henry Ward Beecher

The energy of the mind is the essence of life.

— *Aristotle*

How very little can be done under the spirit of fear.

— *Florence Nightingale*

Life is not a matter of holding good cards, but of playing a poor hand well.

— *Robert Louis Stevenson*

Fortune favors the bold.

— Virgil

Who knows, the mind has the key to all things besides.

— Amos Bronson Alcott

That which does not kill us makes us stronger.

— *Friedrich Nietzsche*

With self-discipline most anything is possible.

— *Theodore Roosevelt*

Knowing is not enough; we must apply. Willing is not enough; we must do.

— *Johann Wolfgang von Goethe*

A gentle word, a kind look, a good-natured smile can work wonders and
accomplish miracles.

— *William Hazlitt*

No man is an island, entire of itself; every man is a piece of the continent.

— *John Donne*

If you want the present to be different from the past, study the past.

— *Baruch Spinoza*

If there is no struggle, there is no progress.

— *Frederick Douglass*

Without craftsmanship, inspiration is a mere reed shaken in the wind.

— *Johannes Brahms*

Tears of joy are like the summer rain drops pierced by sunbeams.

— *Hosea Ballou*

Grace is the beauty of form under the influence of freedom.

— *Friedrich Schiller*

As people are walking all the time, in the same spot, a path appears.

— *John Locke*

To the mind that is still, the whole universe surrenders.

— *Lao Tzu*

Remember when life's path is steep to keep your mind even.

— *Horace*

Ask me not what I have, but what I am.

— *Heinrich Heine*

Great thoughts speak only to the thoughtful mind, but great actions speak to all mankind.

— *Theodore Roosevelt*

It is our attitude at the beginning of a difficult task which, more than anything else, will affect its successful outcome.

— *William James*

Be as you wish to seem.

— *Socrates*

45

It is costly wisdom that is bought by experience.

— *Roger Ascham*

A thousand words will not leave so deep an impression as one deed.

— *Henrik Ibsen*

All experience is an arch, to build upon.

— *Henry Adams*

Thank God every morning when you get up that you have something to do that day, which must be done, whether you like it or not.

— *James Russell Lowell*

Keep your face always toward the sunshine - and shadows will fall behind you.

— Walt Whitman

Creativity is not the finding of a thing, but the making something out
of it after it is found.

— *James Russell Lowell*

We consume our tomorrows fretting about our yesterdays.

— *Persius*

Talking with a friend is nothing else but thinking aloud.

— *Joseph Addison*

You cannot do a kindness too soon, for you never know how soon it will be too late.

— Ralph Waldo Emerson

Genius is the ability to renew one's emotions in daily experience.

— *Paul Cezanne*

Begin, be bold and venture to be wise.

— *Horace*

Life is the flower for which love is the honey.

— *Victor Hugo*

Let the beauty of what you love be what you do.

— *Rumi*

If we learn not humility, we learn nothing.

— *John Jewel*

If there is no struggle, there is no progress.

— *Frederick Douglass*

Write it on your heart that every day is the best day in the year.

— *Ralph Waldo Emerson*

The art of being wise is the art of knowing what to overlook.

— *William James*

They succeed, because they think they can.

— *Virgil*

Success consists of getting up just one more time than you fall.

— *Oliver Goldsmith*

Good actions give strength to ourselves and inspire good actions in others.

— *Plato*

He that humbleth himself wishes to be exalted.

— *Friedrich Nietzsche*

Endure the present, and watch for better things.

— *Virgil*

Do not fear mistakes. You will know failure. Continue to reach out.

— *Benjamin Franklin*

The things that we love tell us what we are.

— *Thomas Aquinas*

Personality is everything in art and poetry.

— *Johann Wolfgang von Goethe*

Friends are the sunshine of life.

— *John Hay*

71

Friends show their love in times of trouble, not in happiness.

— *Euripides*

Good means not merely not to do wrong, but rather not to desire to do wrong.

— *Democritus*

It's not what you look at that matters, it's what you see.

— *Henry David Thoreau*

The true method of knowledge is experiment.

— *William Blake*

Little minds are interested in the extraordinary; great minds in the commonplace.

— *Elbert Hubbard*

What worries you, masters you.

— *John Locke*

The pen is the tongue of the mind.

— *Horace*

When the mind is thinking it is talking to itself.

— *Plato*

Nothing is so good as it seems beforehand.

— *George Eliot*

That which we obtain too easily, we esteem too lightly.

— *Thomas Paine*

Absence sharpens love, presence strengthens it.

— *Thomas Fuller*

All experience is an arch, to build upon.

— *Henry Adams*

All things are difficult before they are easy.

— *Thomas Fuller*

Events will take their course, it is no good of being angry at them; he is happiest who wisely turns them to the best account.

— *Euripides*

There is nothing like a dream to create the future.

— *Victor Hugo*

Positive anything is better than negative nothing.

— *Elbert Hubbard*

There is nothing on this earth more to be prized than true friendship.

— *Thomas Aquinas*

That man is a success who has lived well, laughed often and loved much.

— *Robert Louis Stevenson*

Genius is the ability to renew one's emotions in daily experience.

— Paul Cezanne

The strongest principle of growth lies in the human choice.

— *George Eliot*

You must accept the truth from whatever source it comes.

— *Maimonides*

To every action there is always opposed an equal reaction.

— *Isaac Newton*

Our opportunities to do good are our talents.

— *Cotton Mather*

Doubt comes in at the window when inquiry is denied at the door.

— *Benjamin Jowett*

No man is an island, entire of itself; every man is a piece of the continent.

— *John Donne*

Wonder is the desire for knowledge.

— *Thomas Aquinas*

Make it your habit not to be critical about small things.

— *Edward Everett Hale*

Good actions give strength to ourselves and inspire good actions in others.

— *Plato*

A gentle word, a kind look, a good-natured smile can work wonders and accomplish miracles.

— *William Hazlitt*

A thing is worth what it can do for you, not what you choose to pay for it.

— *John Ruskin*

Excessive fear is always powerless. — *Aeschylus*

Don't judge each day by the harvest you reap but by the seeds that you plant.

— *Robert Louis Stevenson*

Our life is what our thoughts make it.

— *Marcus Aurelius*

Please all, and you will please none.

— *Aesop*

To seek the highest good is to live well.

— Saint Augustine

Beauty is everywhere a welcome guest.

— *Johann Wolfgang von Goethe*

Sooner or later everyone sits down to a banquet of consequences.

— *Robert Louis Stevenson*

The future is purchased by the present.

— *Samuel Johnson*

Do something wonderful, people may imitate it. — *Albert Schweitzer*

Made in the USA
Coppell, TX
08 May 2022

77570240R00063